HORSE
&PONY
BREEDS

HORSE & PONY BREEDS

Carolyn Henderson

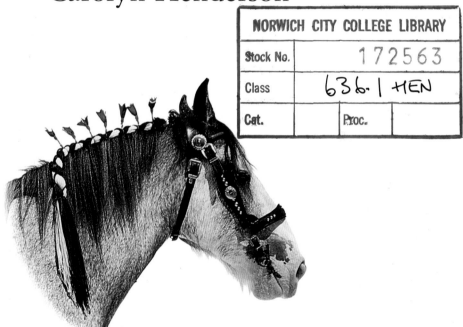

DORLING KINDERSLEY
London • New York • Sydney • Moscow
www.dk.com

A DORLING KINDERSLEY BOOK
www.dk.com

Project Editor Claire Bampton
Project Art Editor Lesley Betts

For Dorling Kindersley
Series Editor Maggie Crowley
Series Art Editor Sharon Grant

DTP Designer Nomazwe Madonko
Production Lisa Moss
Picture Research Francis Vargo
Jacket Design Margherita Gianni

Managing Editor Jayne Parsons
Managing Art Editor Gill Shaw

First published in Great Britain in 1999 by
Dorling Kindersley Limited
9 Henrietta Street, London WC2E 8PS
2 4 6 8 10 9 7 5 3 1

ISBN 0 7513 5887 8

Colour reproduction by Colourscan, Singapore
Printed and bound in Italy by L.E.G.O.

CONTENTS

FOREWORD

ALL HORSES AND PONIES are wonderful animals, from beautiful Thoroughbred racehorses to tiny ponies and the powerful heavy horses. Everyone has their favourite – hopefully you'll find yours in this book. You'll also discover the fascinating story of how the horse developed, why different breeds and types are used for different jobs, and learn about the special qualities of each breed. My first pony was an agile Welsh Section B and since then I've owned and ridden many different breeds. They are all fascinating in their own way and I hope you enjoy learning about them in this book.

ORIGINS

THERE ARE MORE than 75 breeds of horses and ponies. All can be traced back to the same ancestors that appeared on Earth c.55 million years ago. By the time the horse was domesticated about 6,000 years ago, there were four types of horses. From these types developed certain breeds such as the Arab, which have had a great impact on the development of modern horses.

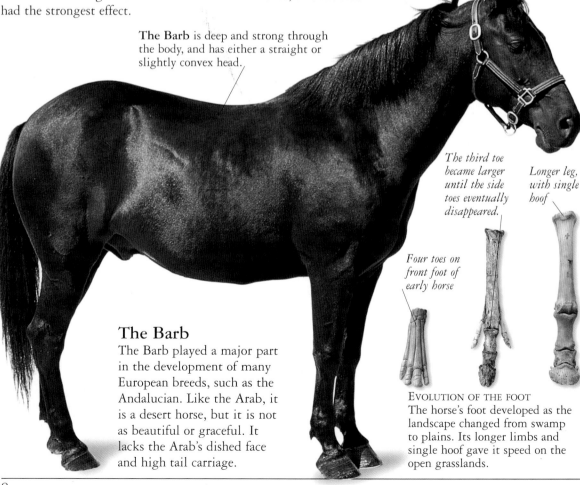

THE FIRST HORSE
Eohippus, or the Dawn Horse, was about 36 cm (14 in) high. It had four toes on each front foot, and three on the hind foot. *Eohippus* fed on leaves, since there was no grass.

The greatest influences

The three main influences on modern riding horses and ponies are the Arab, the Barb, and the Thoroughbred. The Arab and the Barb are the oldest of these, though scientists are not sure which came first. The Thoroughbred is the most recent influence, and has also had the strongest effect.

The Barb is deep and strong through the body, and has either a straight or slightly convex head.

The third toe became larger until the side toes eventually disappeared.

Longer leg, with single hoof

Four toes on front foot of early horse

The Barb

The Barb played a major part in the development of many European breeds, such as the Andalucian. Like the Arab, it is a desert horse, but it is not as beautiful or graceful. It lacks the Arab's dished face and high tail carriage.

EVOLUTION OF THE FOOT
The horse's foot developed as the landscape changed from swamp to plains. Its longer limbs and single hoof gave it speed on the open grasslands.

Dense coat protects against cold and wet.

EXMOOR

Heavy build helps to cope with cold and frost.

Coarser limbs and feathers

HIGHLAND

Thin neck is set very high and supports head with fine ears.

This type had a long, narrow body and was lean and thin-skinned.

AKHAL-TEKE

Refined build and slim body

Dished head, characteristics of both the Arab and Caspian pony

CASPIAN

Pony type 1

Found in north-west Europe, this pony type was about 12.2 hh. It had a straight profile and small ears. This hardy pony was highly resistant to wet and able to thrive in harsh conditions. The Exmoor pony is its nearest modern equivalent.

Pony type 2

Standing at about 14.2 hh, this type was heavily built and coarse in appearance. Its head was large in relation to its body. This pony settled in northern Eurasia, where it was able to survive the cold. The Highland pony is its nearest equivalent.

Horse type 3

A horse rather than a pony, this horse type stood at about 15 hh. It had a long body, long neck, and long ears and was shallow through the girth. Living in central Asia, it was resistant to heat and drought. The Akhal-Teke is the modern breed that resembles it most closely.

Horse type 4

This type was a pony in terms of height, but a miniature horse in terms of conformation. It had a "dished" face and a high tail carriage. A dished face is a characteristic of both the Arab and Caspian pony; some scientists believe that horse type 4 was the blueprint for these breeds.

THE MODERN HORSE

MODERN HORSES and ponies are bred for specific functions. These range from pleasure riding, driving, and working on the land, to competing in specialist sports such as dressage, racing, and showjumping. Horses can be classified by breed, type, colour, and markings. A horse bred for one type of activity may not be suitable for another. Some, however, are adaptable and have many uses.

Warmbloods

Warmbloods are the ultimate modern sports horses. They combine Thoroughbred, or hot blood, with cold blood, or heavier horse, influences. Warmbloods are the result of careful breeding programmes.

Performance horses are used to breed warmbloods.

Classification of the horse

The two main types of horse are heavy and light. Ponies form a third group. Heavy horses include the largest, most powerful breeds, and often stand at more than 17 hh. Light horse breeds and types, such as riding horses, stand at more than 14.2 hh, while ponies stand at 14.2 hh or less.

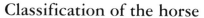

CLYDESDALE

Plaited mane is traditional.

Powerful hindquarters for speed

Well-proportioned hindlegs

HEAVY HORSES
Heavy breeds are the giants of the horse world. They have been bred to work on the land and have broad, strong backs and powerful legs. The angle of the shoulder is often straighter than in light horse breeds, which gives the heavier horses great pulling power.

Feather protects skin on powerful forelegs when plodding through muddy land.

COLOURS AND MARKINGS

Colours and markings are key identification points for horses and ponies. Colours can be solid or broken, and some horses, such as palominos, are bred specifically for their colour. Face and leg markings are white patches on a solid colour, such as chestnut.

COLOURS

COAT COLOURINGS
Colour is determined by the horse's genetic make-up. Some colours are always dominant. For example, if one parent is grey and the other is either bay, black, or chestnut, the foal will always be grey. There are also classifications within the colours, so a skewbald may be called a tobiano or an overo depending on the distribution of solid colour compared to white.

DUN

PALOMINO

PIEBALD

SPOTTED

CHESTNUT

SKEWBALD

BAY

DAPPLE GREY

MARKINGS

FACE AND LEG MARKINGS
The most common face markings are stars, stripes, snips, or combinations of these. A white or bald face covers the forehead and front of the face. Leg markings include socks, which extend up to the knees, while stockings run further up the leg.

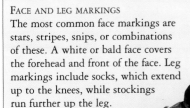

STRIPE

STAR

STOCKING

SOCK

ERMINE

THOROUGHBRED

Fine coat and slender build help horse to stay cool.

Bushy mane protects pony against cold and wet weather.

WELSH PONY

Long, sloping shoulder indicates good movement and a comfortable ride.

Body is compact with depth through the girth.

LIGHT HORSE
The light horse riding breeds and types always have some Thoroughbred blood. Their body shape and movement makes them comfortable to ride.

PONY
Different pony breeds have height restrictions and definite characteristics depending on the type of work for which they were traditionally used. Many are tough and hardy.

Short forearms help bear weight.

PHYSICAL FEATURES

THE HORSE HAS acute senses, which, together with its physical characteristics and shape, enable it to spot potential dangers and flee. Correct conformation, or shape, is not just important because it makes the horse beautiful; if the horse's body and legs have the right proportions and angles, it will be more likely to stay sound and be athletic. No horse is perfect, but its strengths should outweigh its weaknesses.

Conformation

A well-made horse has good hooves and legs to support its body easily. Its back, quarters, and hindlegs should be strong, and its body deep for efficient heart and lung function. A sloping shoulder angle helps the riding horse move gracefully.

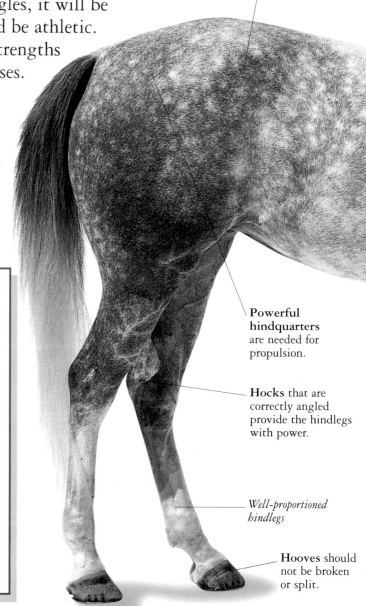

Strong loins and back give strength. The back must not be too long or too short.

Powerful hindquarters are needed for propulsion.

Hocks that are correctly angled provide the hindlegs with power.

Well-proportioned hindlegs

Hooves should not be broken or split.

How to measure a horse
Stand a horse on level ground so that its hooves are square and its head and neck are at a natural angle. Measure from the highest part of the withers down to the ground. Horses are traditionally measured in hands and inches.

A hand is 10 cm (4 in).

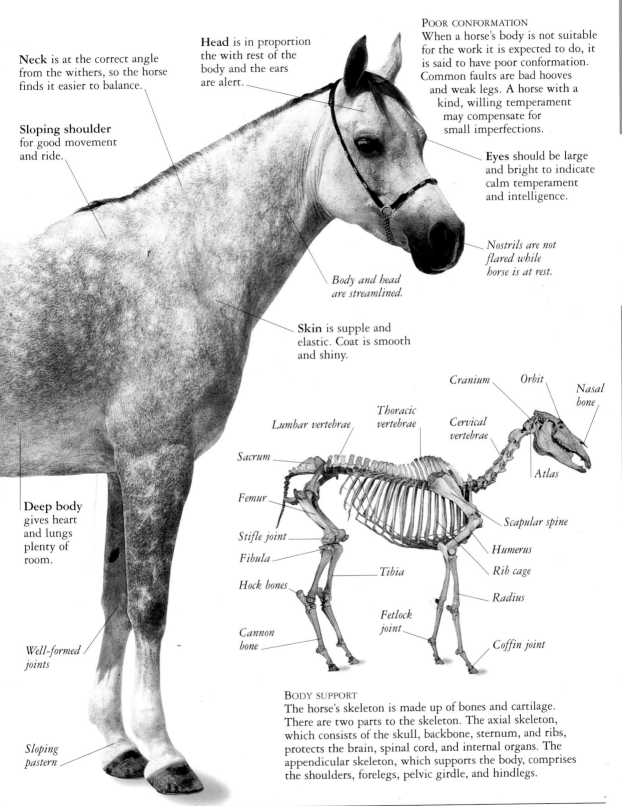

Neck is at the correct angle from the withers, so the horse finds it easier to balance.

Head is in proportion the with rest of the body and the ears are alert.

POOR CONFORMATION
When a horse's body is not suitable for the work it is expected to do, it is said to have poor conformation. Common faults are bad hooves and weak legs. A horse with a kind, willing temperament may compensate for small imperfections.

Sloping shoulder for good movement and ride.

Eyes should be large and bright to indicate calm temperament and intelligence.

Nostrils are not flared while horse is at rest.

Body and head are streamlined.

Skin is supple and elastic. Coat is smooth and shiny.

Deep body gives heart and lungs plenty of room.

Well-formed joints

Sloping pastern

Cranium   *Orbit*   *Nasal bone*

Thoracic vertebrae

Cervical vertebrae

Lumbar vertebrae

Sacrum

Atlas

Femur

Scapular spine

Stifle joint

Humerus

Fibula

Rib cage

Tibia

Radius

Hock bones

Fetlock joint

Cannon bone

Coffin joint

BODY SUPPORT
The horse's skeleton is made up of bones and cartilage. There are two parts to the skeleton. The axial skeleton, which consists of the skull, backbone, sternum, and ribs, protects the brain, spinal cord, and internal organs. The appendicular skeleton, which supports the body, comprises the shoulders, forelegs, pelvic girdle, and hindlegs.

HORSE AND PONY TYPES

HORSES CAN BE classified by type as well as breed. Sometimes a horse's breeding is unspecific, but its conformation, build, and movement make it a particular type. Types have a set of physical characteristics that help them perform specific functions, such as hunting, hacking, or farming. However, some breeds have a powerful influence on types. For example, Thoroughbred blood gives quality and extra agility to riding and sport horses, while most cobs have some draught horse ancestry.

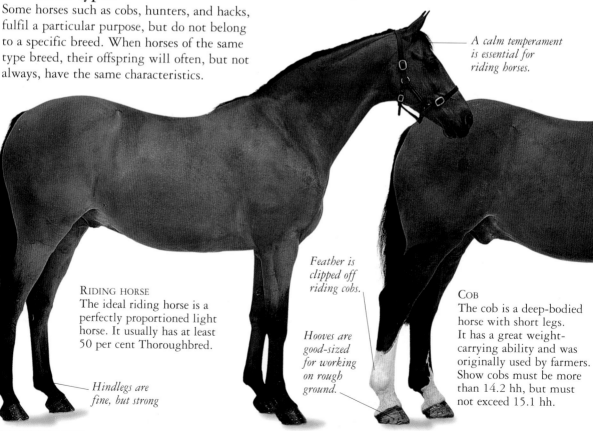

Domestic horses
For many centuries, all horses were wild. They were not domesticated until about 6,000 years ago. Today, although the Camargue horses of southern France live in the wild, they are kept in herds and used to work the area's black cattle. The only truly wild horse is Przewalski's horse.

Different types
Some horses such as cobs, hunters, and hacks, fulfil a particular purpose, but do not belong to a specific breed. When horses of the same type breed, their offspring will often, but not always, have the same characteristics.

A calm temperament is essential for riding horses.

RIDING HORSE
The ideal riding horse is a perfectly proportioned light horse. It usually has at least 50 per cent Thoroughbred.

Hindlegs are fine, but strong

Feather is clipped off riding cobs.

Hooves are good-sized for working on rough ground.

COB
The cob is a deep-bodied horse with short legs. It has a great weight-carrying ability and was originally used by farmers. Show cobs must be more than 14.2 hh, but must not exceed 15.1 hh.

Fairly long, well-muscled neck is important for balance.

Elegant frame is combined with a fine coat.

Long forearms for good movement and strength.

Hindlegs and hindquarters are powerful for quick turns and acceleration.

Joints and legs that are clean and strong enable horse to run far and fast.

POLO PONY
Horses used for polo are always called ponies. Most are between 15 hh and 15.3 hh. Thoroughbreds crossed with Argentinian Criollo ponies are popular breeds for polo.

THOROUGHBRED
Although not strictly a type, the Thoroughbred has more influence than any other breed on the modern types of horse. It is the fastest of the breeds and gives physical quality to any breed or type with which it is crossed.

Mane traditionally clipped

A short, powerful neck supports a noble head.

Hunters must be fit and strong.

Well-sloped shoulders are perfect for galloping and jumping.

Short, strong forelegs carry weight.

HUNTER
The hunter is a powerful horse, that is able to gallop and jump well. It is often a combination of Thoroughbred and draught horse, such as the Irish Draught.

Joints act as shock absorbers.

Forelegs take the strain when jumping and galloping.

WORK AND PLEASURE

THE HORSE'S ROLE has changed dramatically since its domestication 6,000 years ago. Once used for work on the land and as a means of transport, the horse now has a much wider use as a pleasure and sports animal. Modern technology means that machinery has made many working horses redundant, but as long as there are areas that can only be reached on horseback, horses will always be needed.

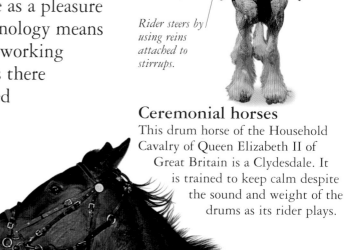

Rider steers by using reins attached to stirrups.

Ceremonial horses

This drum horse of the Household Cavalry of Queen Elizabeth II of Great Britain is a Clydesdale. It is trained to keep calm despite the sound and weight of the drums as its rider plays.

Sports horses

Sports horses are the athletes of the horse world and are bred and trained to take part in a range of sports. Horse sports include racing, dressage, showjumping, eventing, and endurance. At top-level competition, the training, selling, and breeding of horses has become big business.

Horse is encouraged to hold its head high.

Harness horses wear special bits to give the driver control and steering.

RACEHORSES

Racehorses are the most valuable horses in the world. The Thoroughbred racing industry is the largest, but harness and Arab racing also offer huge prizes. It is possible to compete in racing as an amateur rider or driver, but many races are ridden by professionals.

Pacers move legs in lateral pairs (on the same side).

Military horses

Horses are trained for military purposes in some parts of the world, such as Afghanistan. They carry riders and packs across territory that cannot be reached by vehicles.

Military horses, such as these from the US, are bold but calm.

Remote war zones, such as Afghanistan, demand horsepower.

WAR HORSES

Horses have always been used in war. In ancient times they pulled chariots to allow men to travel faster than on foot. Later, armed riders, called cavalry, were introduced and the horse played a major part in wars until just after World War I, when mechanized vehicles took over.

MOUNTED POLICE

Police horses are rigorously trained to accept loud noises and frightening hazards before they are allow to perform regular duties, such as street patrols and crowd control. They must prove that they are steady in traffic and reliable in crowd situations.

Helmet and goggles are worn for safety.

Silks come in a variety of colours.

Driving in harness racing takes as much skill and courage as riding racehorses. Falls are even more dangerous.

Drivers are not allowed to misuse the whip.

Strong hindquarters are essential to harness racing horses.

Light, spoked wheels with air-filled tyres

AMERICAN STANDARDBRED

HARNESS RACING

American Standardbreds are the stars of harness racing. Horses pull a sulky (two-wheeled vehicle for one person) and trot as fast as many other racehorses gallop. Some harness racers are trained to pace, so that their legs move in lateral pairs.

THE ARAB

THE ARAB is one of the oldest breeds and is often described as the most beautiful horse in the world. It is easily recognized by its short, refined head and high tail carriage. When crossed with other breeds, these characteristics are often passed on, though to a lesser extent. Tough, hardy, and fast, the Arab excels in racing and endurance sports. It is sensitive and intelligent.

Legends and history

The Arab can be traced back 3,000 years, although legend says it was created by Allah from handfuls of the north and south winds. Bedouin tribesmen allowed their favourite Arab mares to live in their tents. Artists have always been captivated by the Arab's beauty.

Arab versatility

Arabs are hardy and athletic horses with naturally good balance. They are not fashionable for dressage because of their high head and tail carriage, but can perform difficult movements as well as any other breed. Their long stride, great speed, and tough hooves make them naturally good at endurance sports.

High-set tail

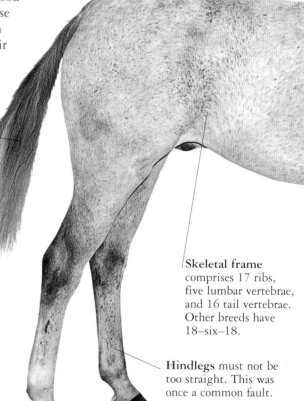

THE ARAB

- Seventeen ribs compared to 18 in other breeds, so it is short-backed
- Bone is denser and stronger than in other breeds
- Mane and tail hair is fine and very silky
- Colours are grey, bay, chestnut, and black
- Muzzle is small with large, flared nostrils
- Legs are long and slender

Skeletal frame comprises 17 ribs, five lumbar vertebrae, and 16 tail vertebrae. Other breeds have 18–six–18.

Hindlegs must not be too straight. This was once a common fault.

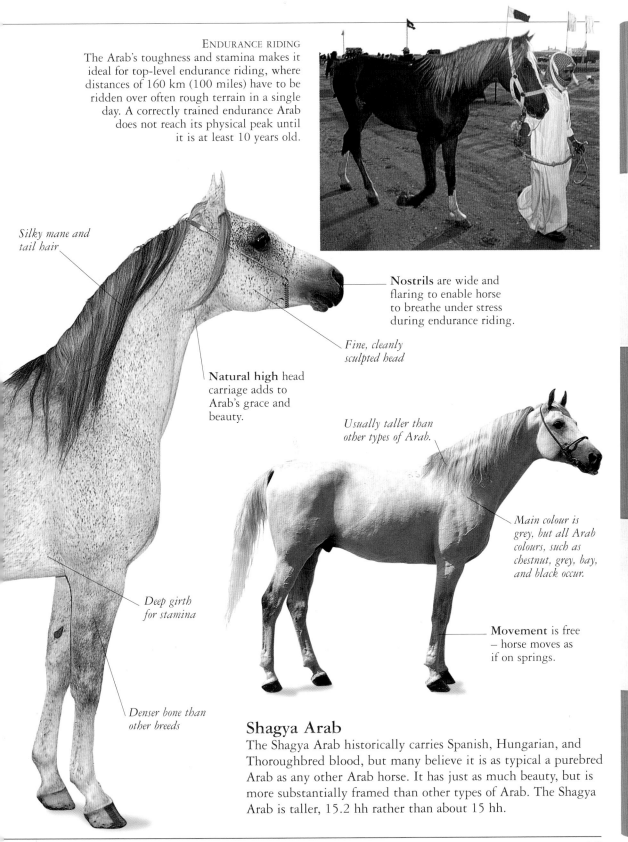

The Arab's toughness and stamina makes it ideal for top-level endurance riding, where distances of 160 km (100 miles) have to be ridden over often rough terrain in a single day. A correctly trained endurance Arab does not reach its physical peak until it is at least 10 years old.

Silky mane and tail hair

Nostrils are wide and flaring to enable horse to breathe under stress during endurance riding.

Fine, cleanly sculpted head

Natural high head carriage adds to Arab's grace and beauty.

Usually taller than other types of Arab.

Main colour is grey, but all Arab colours, such as chestnut, grey, bay, and black occur.

Deep girth for stamina

Movement is free – horse moves as if on springs.

Denser bone than other breeds

Shagya Arab

The Shagya Arab historically carries Spanish, Hungarian, and Thoroughbred blood, but many believe it is as typical a purebred Arab as any other Arab horse. It has just as much beauty, but is more substantially framed than other types of Arab. The Shagya Arab is taller, 15.2 hh rather than about 15 hh.

SPANISH HORSES

THE ANDALUCIAN, which has been known for centuries as the Spanish horse, is the third greatest influence on modern horse and pony breeds. Its beauty and power, combined with a bold but willing temperament, have made it the mount of bullfighters, classical dressage riders, and enthusiasts throughout the world. The Lusitano and the Lipizzaner also have strong Spanish influences.

HARNESS CHAMPIONS
The Andalucian, Lusitano, and Lipizzaner are all spectacular carriage horses and are also highly prized as riding horses. Their good movement is combined with a trainable temperament.

The Andalucian

The Andalucian is a powerful horse with a substantial frame that makes it look bigger than its average 15.2 hh. Its movement is controlled and high stepping. Strong hindquarters give it a natural ability for advanced dressage movements.

Hindquarters are particularly strong.

Coat colour is usually grey or bay.

Powerful hock joints add strength.

Knee joints should be large and flat for soundness and toughness.

Tail is long, luxurious, and often wavy.

SPANISH HORSES

- Once unfashionable, these breeds are now finding favour with some dressage riders

- All three breeds are usually grey

- Kind temperament means that stallions are favoured for riding

- Mares are traditionally used only for breeding

- The Alter Real is a breed that also descends from Andalucian stock

---

The Lipizzaner

The Lipizzaner is most famous as the dancing white horse of the Spanish Riding School in Vienna. During the war in Bosnia and Croatia in the 1990s, Lipizzaners at the former State Stud in Bosnia were saved by an international rescue operation, thus preserving valuable bloodlines. The horses have been bred at this stud for 400 years.

Horses at the Spanish Riding School are all Lipizzaner stallions.

Lipizzaners are grey, but are dark when born.

The levade is one of the movements performed by the talented Spanish Riding School horses.

Spanish Riding School's riders are all men who must reach a high standard on schooled stallions before being allowed to train young ones.

Powerful, crested neck with silky and often wavy mane.

Handsome, straight profile

Short back and good loin

Profile is straight like that of the Andalucian.

Brand denotes bloodlines and stud of origin.

Coat can come in all colours but is mainly grey.

The Lusitano

The Portuguese Lusitano, developed from the Andalucian, has a slight Arab influence, but is longer and lighter in the limbs. Highly-schooled Lusitanos are ridden by Portuguese bullfighters, called "rejoneadores".

Cannon bone is particularly long.

THOROUGHBRED

THE THOROUGHBRED EVOLVED during the 17th and 18th centuries. It is the fastest and most valuable breed in the world, and is often crossed with other breeds to improve their quality. Thoroughbreds are generally bred for racing, but are also successful in horse trials and other sports.

Anglo-Arab

The Anglo-Arab is a cross between the two most influential breeds in the world, the Thoroughbred and the Arab. It looks like the Thoroughbred in appearance, but ideally it should combine the speed of the Thoroughbred with the toughness of the Arab, and share the beauty of both.

Thoroughbred

The Thoroughbred has had a strong influence on all breeds of modern sport horse. The best have great courage, mental stamina, and speed. They can be highly strung and can sometimes have difficult temperaments.

Fine, silky hair in mane, tail, and coat

ANGLO-ARAB

THOROUGHBRED

SOUND AND TOUGH
The best Anglo-Arabs have strong limbs and feet that are able to withstand hard work.

DEEP GIRTH
The Thoroughbred should have a deep girth. This allows for its lungs to expand fully when the horse is galloping.

Born to race

The Thoroughbred is built for speed. There are two different types: flat racehorses are usually more finely built and race as two and three-year-olds. Steeplechasers race over fences and do not start until they are four years old. Their racing careers last much longer than flat racehorses, sometimes until they are about 13 years old.

American Standardbred

The Standardbred is America's own racing breed. Its breeding has Thoroughbred influence from the 18th century. It is a harness racing horse that pulls a special lightweight vehicle, usually over distances of 1.6 km (one mile). The breed's name comes from the 19th century, when horses had to meet a standard time in races to enter the breed register.

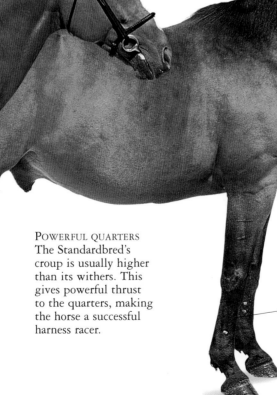

Lower-set neck can be stretched out in a racing finish.

POWERFUL QUARTERS
The Standardbred's croup is usually higher than its withers. This gives powerful thrust to the quarters, making the horse a successful harness racer.

Colours are mainly bay, as here, brown, black, and chestnut.

Strong limbs reduce the risk of injury when the horse is racing at speed.

AMERICAN STANDARDBRED

MOUNTAIN AND MOORLAND PONIES

MOUNTAIN AND MOORLAND ponies are able to survive harsh living conditions. They first came from the British Isles, where they are native ponies, but are now bred all over the world. They can carry heavy weights for their size, and the larger breeds can be ridden by adults or children. They are often crossed with Thoroughbreds to produce sport horses.

Moorland ponies
The Exmoor is a rare breed. It has a fan of hair at the top of the tail, called an ice tail, which protects it from bad weather. Another moorland pony, the Dartmoor pony, is more elegant than the Exmoor.

Exmoors are always bay, brown, or dun.

Small breeds
Dartmoor, Exmoor, Shetland, and Welsh A and B ponies are small but strong. Their kind temperaments and athletic abilities make them good to ride if trained correctly. They also make sound driving ponies.

WELSH SECTION A

Head has intelligent expression and small pointed ears.

Double layered coat in winter protects pony against harsh weather.

Neck is not too long and is slightly arched.

Bodies should be strong and deep.

This breed can be any colour except piebald or skewbald.

Tough hooves mean they do not always need shoes.

Short cannons

SHETLAND
The Shetland is the smallest British native pony breed, and originated from the bleak Shetland Islands off the coast of Scotland, UK. Its average height is 1 m (40 in), and it is the only breed that is not measured in hands.

WELSH PONIES
The Welsh Section A, or Welsh Mountain pony, is particularly well-proportioned and elegant. The Section B, or Welsh pony, is slightly stockier.

Large breeds

The larger native breeds are bred as performance ponies for children and adults. The Connemara and Welsh Section D are the most popular and are often good jumpers.

Long neck and good shoulder make a comfortable ride.

Usual colours are bay, brown, and chestnut.

Strong hocks and hindquarters for powerful stride.

Connemara is usually grey, dun, or bay.

NEW FOREST
New Forest ponies have been influenced by the introduction of Welsh and Thoroughbred blood. They are sure-footed and have kind temperaments.

WELSH SECTION D
Also called the Welsh Cob, this pony is the largest British native breed and can be over 15 hh. It often has a powerful trot.

CONNEMARA
Originally bred in Ireland and popular throughout the world, the Connemara has a range of uses from dressage to jumping.

Strong back and hindquarters for carrying weight.

FELL

Tails and manes are uncut.

Coat is usually dun or grey in colour.

Fine, silky feather on lower legs.

FELL AND DALES
The Fell and Dales ponies look similar, although the Fell is slightly smaller and lighter in build. Both are usually black, brown, or bay and have thick, silky leg feather.

HIGHLAND
The Highland pony is very strong and can carry a weight of up to 18 stone (126 kg). It often has a dark stripe, called an eel stripe, down the centre of its back.

EUROPEAN PONIES

EUROPEAN PONIES might not be as well-known worldwide as British native ponies, but their popularity is growing fast. Haflingers and Fjords, in particular, make good riding and driving ponies, and are prized as purebreds rather than as possible crosses with Thoroughbreds. The Haflinger has influenced the Italian Bardigiano, while the Fjord resembles the Highland pony.

Pony power

Many European ponies are kept for work as well as for pleasure. They are usually strong and sturdy, which makes them ideal for harness work in mountainous areas. They also thrive in harsh conditions, and are less expensive to feed than large horses.

Bardigiano

The Bardigiano is an Italian breed of mountain pony. It has been influenced by draught horse blood and by the Avelignese, a pony that is very similar to, but heavier than, the Haflinger.

Coat is often bay or brown, with no white markings.

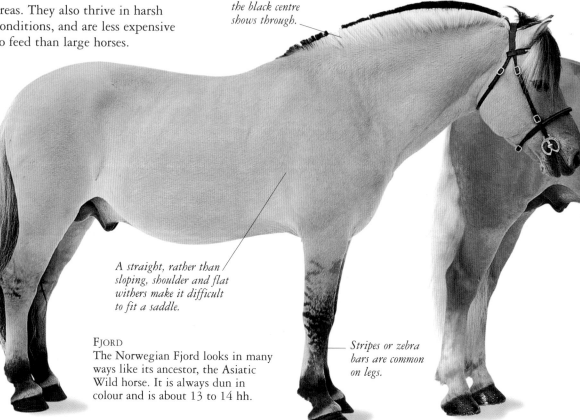

Mane is cut to stand on end, so the black centre shows through.

A straight, rather than sloping, shoulder and flat withers make it difficult to fit a saddle.

FJORD

The Norwegian Fjord looks in many ways like its ancestor, the Asiatic Wild horse. It is always dun in colour and is about 13 to 14 hh.

Stripes or zebra bars are common on legs.

The Piebald Pottok stands up to 13 hh.

A straight back and flat withers are common characteristics.

The shape of the legs is improved by Welsh Section B and Arab blood.

Brown, black, bay, and liver chestnut, often with white markings on the head, are the most common colours.

POTTOK
The Pottok is a semi-wild pony from the Basque region of France. There are three types: the Standard, the Piebald, and the Double.

LANDAIS
The Landais is an established French pony breed with Welsh and Arab influence. It is hardy and willing, and stands between about 11 and 13.2 hh.

Thick, flaxen mane, like tail

Open nostrils for easy breathing in oxygen-poor mountain air.

HAFLINGER
The Austrian Haflinger is always chestnut or palomino and ranges from 13.2 to 15 hh. It is the most attractive and adaptable of the European breeds.

SNOW PONIES
Sleighs pulled by Haflingers are a special attraction in the Austrian mountains. Ponies are not put in a harness until they are four years old, and many work until they are about 30.

PONIES WORLDWIDE

ALL PONIES AND horses are bred to carry out specific tasks. As the type of work ponies are bred for changes, so do the qualities and characteristics that breeders aim for. This has led to the creation of new breeds, such as the Pony of the Americas, and miniature breeds, such as the Falabella. Some breeds for example the Caspian are kept for riding, others such as the American Shetland are used for driving, and some like the Bashkir even provide milk.

Small and beautiful

Falabellas and miniature Shetlands are bred to be as small as possible. They are too small to be ridden, and some people believe that this is wrong. There is certainly a danger that breeding to create a small animal increases the risk of weakness, such as loss of strength and a poor constitution.

FALABELLA
The Falabella takes its name from an Argentinian family that developed the breed. It is really a horse but is never more than 76 cm (30 in) tall and it is generally called a pony.

Pony of the Americas
The Pony of the Americas was first bred in 1954 and is a cross between a Shetland and an Appaloosa. It is now a recognized breed, prized for its spotted coat and its suitability as a riding pony.

The pony's height is set between 11.2 and 13.2 hh.

Back is straight and tail carried high.

Perfectly proportioned head

Luxurious tail growth, like mane

Fine coat offers little protection against harsh weather.

CASPIAN
The Caspian is probably a forerunner of the Arabian horse. It is an elegant riding pony, suitable for small children, and it stands between 10 and 12 hh.

Short back and strong hindquarters

Flared nostrils and short ears are characteristic of this breed.

Curly coat can be clipped and spun into coarse cloth.

Long legs can be a weakness, but the Timor is sure-footed.

Hard hooves do not need to be shod.

Bashkir

The Bashkir is a Russian breed famed for its curly coat. It is a stocky pony of about 14 hh which can withstand sub-zero temperatures.

Timor

Named after the Indonesian island where it originated, the Timor stands between 9 and 11 hh. It is usually bay, black, or brown and is sure-footed and agile.

Well-shaped withers

Long neck

Tail, and mane, hair is fine and silky.

AMERICAN SHETLAND
The American Shetland is very different from the native Shetland pony and has Hackney, Arab, and Thoroughbred blood. It stands about 10.2 hh and is bred to drive.

Trained with weighted shoes to encourage a high-stepping action like that of the Hackney.

WARMBLOODS

THE TERM WARMBLOOD describes horses that are a mixture of either Thoroughbred or Arab, and other breeds. It is also used for European sports horses that have Thoroughbred influence but have been carefully bred. Warmbloods are tested for athleticism, soundness, and good conformation. They now dominate international dressage and showjumping.

Hanoverian

The Hanoverian is the best-known warmblood. Its ancestry can be traced back to 1735 at Celle in Germany. This breed was originally heavier than those today, which have a greater percentage of Thoroughbred blood to give them power and elegance.

Neck is well set and long.

Noble, attractive head

Powerful hindquarters for jumping

Strong back helps the horse perform advanced dressage movements.

Wide, open-angled throat helps the horse to flex and work on the bit when performing.

Dressage demands concentrated and repetitive training.

ATHLETIC AND FLEXIBLE
Good movement is the secret of the Hanoverian's success and popularity. Its strong back and hindquarters give it the power required for dressage and jumping.

Better-shaped hooves than original examples of the breed.

DRESSAGE
The Hanoverian's good conformation, controlled movement, and courageous temperament fulfils the demands of top-level dressage.

Back length is in perfect proportion.

Withers and neck angles are ideal for a riding horse.

Thoroughbred blood has improved back conformation.

Powerful shoulders for jumping

Good hooves and forelegs

Danish warmblood

Denmark's sport horse has been developed over the past 30 years by crossing the Frederiksborg, a Danish carriage horse, with Thoroughbred and Thoroughbred crosses. The Danish warmblood is more elegant than the Hanoverian and is renowned for its kind nature.

Dutch warmblood

The Dutch warmblood is a combination of the Gelderlander, a carriage horse breed, the heavy Groningen, and the Thoroughbred. It excels in both showjumping and dressage. Mated with Thoroughbred mares, it produces elegant but powerful offspring.

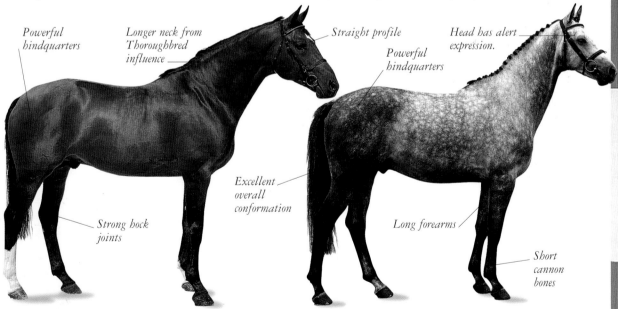

Powerful hindquarters

Longer neck from Thoroughbred influence

Straight profile

Powerful hindquarters

Head has alert expression.

Strong hock joints

Excellent overall conformation

Long forearms

Short cannon bones

Selle Francais

France's warmblood is unique in that its ancestry is with the trotting horse. It has been refined by Thoroughbred and Anglo-Arab blood. The result is a horse that excels mainly at jumping, but has the speed and agility for eventing.

Trakehner

The Trakehner originated in East Prussia, now part of Poland, and is a model of the ideal competition horse. It combines elegance with a substantial frame and its courageous and willing temperament allow it to excel in all areas.

IRISH DRAUGHT AND CLEVELAND BAY

THE IRISH DRAUGHT and Cleveland Bay were originally bred to pull carts. Today these breeds are mainly crossed with Thoroughbreds to produce competition horses. The Irish Draught is a particularly popular influence on horses bred for showjumping and eventing.

TALENT FOR JUMPING
Irish Draught blood breeds many talented showjumpers. Great strength in the hindquarters, agility, and boldness are its hallmarks.

Irish Draught

The Irish Draught is deep-bodied with good legs. Bred for agricultural work, it was also expected to carry Irish farmers out hunting. This helped to develop an athletic, sure-footed horse.

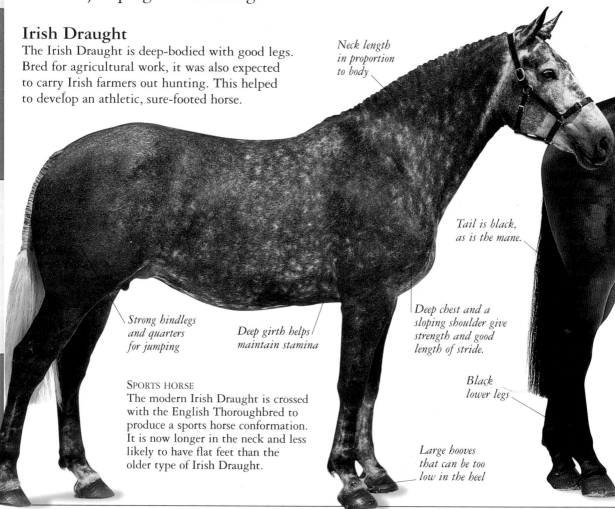

Neck length in proportion to body

Tail is black, as is the mane.

Strong hindlegs and quarters for jumping

Deep girth helps maintain stamina

Deep chest and a sloping shoulder give strength and good length of stride.

Black lower legs

SPORTS HORSE
The modern Irish Draught is crossed with the English Thoroughbred to produce a sports horse conformation. It is now longer in the neck and less likely to have flat feet than the older type of Irish Draught.

Large hooves that can be too low in the heel

Bavarian warmblood

The Cleveland Bay has had a strong influence on the Bavarian warmblood, one of the lesser-known warmblood sports horses. In the 18th century, partbred Cleveland Bay stallions were imported to Bavaria to give greater substance to the horses bred there.

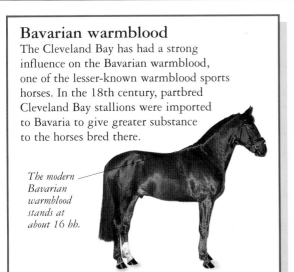

The modern Bavarian warmblood stands at about 16 hh.

CARRIAGE HORSES
The Cleveland Bay has always been a royal carriage horse in the UK, and is still kept by the royal family. Cleveland stock has been sent all over the world, particularly to the US.

Cleveland Bay

This breed is always bay with black points (mane, tail, ear tips, and lower legs). Its head is said to show influence from the Andalucian.

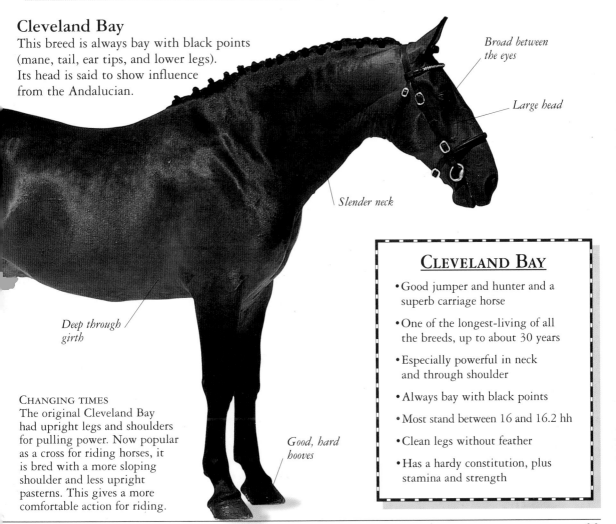

Broad between the eyes

Large head

Slender neck

Deep through girth

Good, hard hooves

CHANGING TIMES
The original Cleveland Bay had upright legs and shoulders for pulling power. Now popular as a cross for riding horses, it is bred with a more sloping shoulder and less upright pasterns. This gives a more comfortable action for riding.

CLEVELAND BAY

- Good jumper and hunter and a superb carriage horse

- One of the longest-living of all the breeds, up to about 30 years

- Especially powerful in neck and through shoulder

- Always bay with black points

- Most stand between 16 and 16.2 hh

- Clean legs without feather

- Has a hardy constitution, plus stamina and strength

HEAVY HORSES

HEAVY HORSES are the giants of the horse world. Bred to work on the land and to pull heavy loads, they are usually not less than 16.2 hh and often reach heights in excess of 17 hh. The oldest heavy horse breed is probably the Ardennais from France and Belgium, which can be traced back more than 2,000 years. The Shire is the best-known heavy horse and is descended from the medieval war horse.

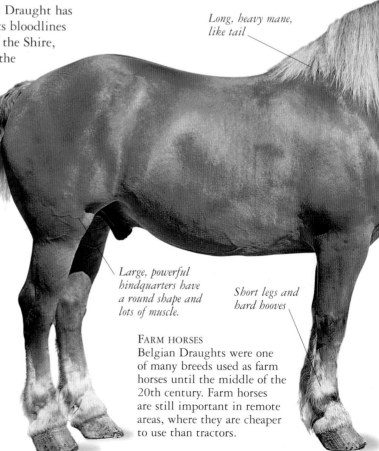

Thick mane

Percherons are often dapple grey.

Percheron
The Percheron is the lightest of the heavy horses, but it is still very powerful. It has no feather and is prized for its calm and pleasant temperament.

Belgian Draught
Also known as the Brabant, the Belgian Draught has had a great influence on other breeds. Its bloodlines have contributed to the development of the Shire, the Clydesdale, the Suffolk Punch, and the Irish Draught. It is bred mainly in Belgium but is popular in the US.

Long, heavy mane, like tail

Tail is traditionally tied up for work.

Funeral horses
The Friesian is the lightest of the coldblooded breeds. It is mainly a harness horse and is popular for pulling hearses because of its black coat. The Friesian can be ridden and has a energetic trot.

The Friesian stands 15 hh and upwards.

Large, powerful hindquarters have a round shape and lots of muscle.

Short legs and hard hooves

FARM HORSES
Belgian Draughts were one of many breeds used as farm horses until the middle of the 20th century. Farm horses are still important in remote areas, where they are cheaper to use than tractors.

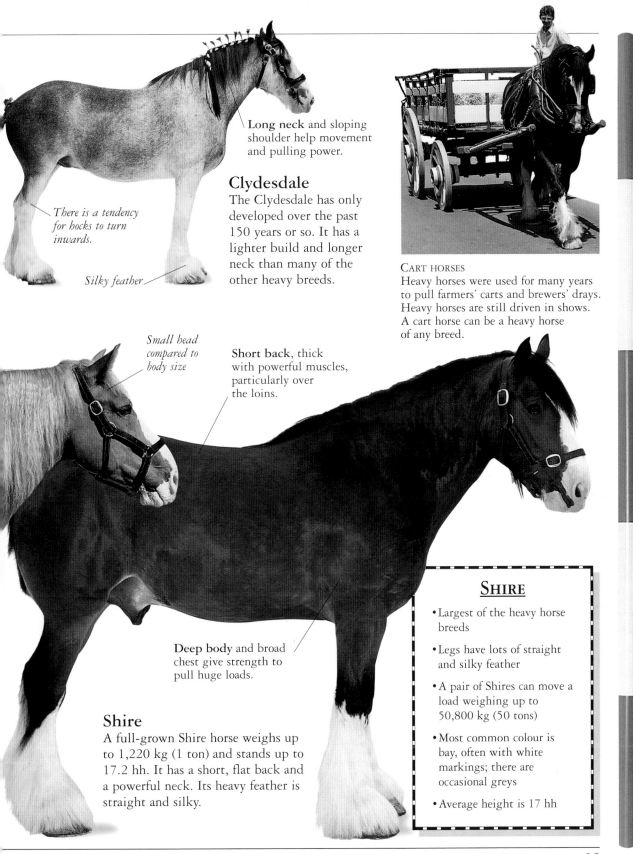

Long neck and sloping shoulder help movement and pulling power.

There is a tendency for hocks to turn inwards.

Silky feather

Clydesdale
The Clydesdale has only developed over the past 150 years or so. It has a lighter build and longer neck than many of the other heavy breeds.

CART HORSES
Heavy horses were used for many years to pull farmers' carts and brewers' drays. Heavy horses are still driven in shows. A cart horse can be a heavy horse of any breed.

Small head compared to body size

Short back, thick with powerful muscles, particularly over the loins.

Deep body and broad chest give strength to pull huge loads.

Shire
A full-grown Shire horse weighs up to 1,220 kg (1 ton) and stands up to 17.2 hh. It has a short, flat back and a powerful neck. Its heavy feather is straight and silky.

SHIRE

- Largest of the heavy horse breeds

- Legs have lots of straight and silky feather

- A pair of Shires can move a load weighing up to 50,800 kg (50 tons)

- Most common colour is bay, often with white markings; there are occasional greys

- Average height is 17 hh

PRIZED FOR COLOUR

MANY HORSES are popular because of their coat colours. They include skewbalds and piebalds, Pintos, Appaloosas, and palominos. Some, such as Appaloosas, are classed as breeds, while others, such as palominos are types. In some breeds and types the colour and pattern of the coat is always the same.

In some countries travellers prefer skewbalds to horses of solid colour.

SKEWBALDS
Skewbalds are brown and white and piebalds are black and white. They were prized by the native Americans.

Spotted horses
Appaloosas are often called spotted horses. There are also spotted ponies. The American Appaloosa was developed by the Nez Percés in the 18th century. The Pony of the Americas is a cross between the Appaloosa and the Shetland.

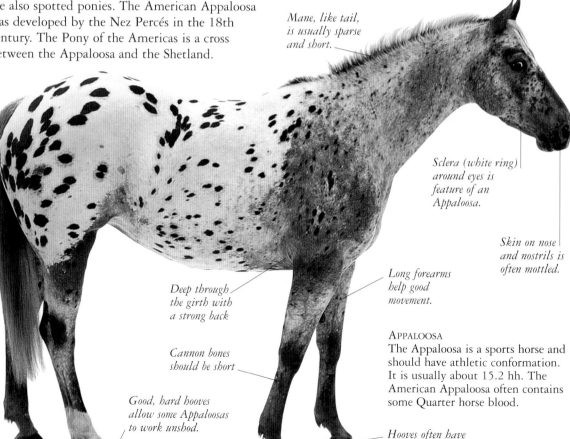

Mane, like tail, is usually sparse and short.

Sclera (white ring) around eyes is feature of an Appaloosa.

Skin on nose and nostrils is often mottled.

Deep through the girth with a strong back

Long forearms help good movement.

Cannon bones should be short

Good, hard hooves allow some Appaloosas to work unshod.

APPALOOSA
The Appaloosa is a sports horse and should have athletic conformation. It is usually about 15.2 hh. The American Appaloosa often contains some Quarter horse blood.

Hooves often have vertical black and white stripes.

Colours not breeds

In most countries, horses such as skewbalds and palominos differ widely in build, from elegant riding horses to cobs and draught animals. They are therefore classed as types, not breeds. In the US, many horses of specific colour are bred to a particular type and are classed as breeds.

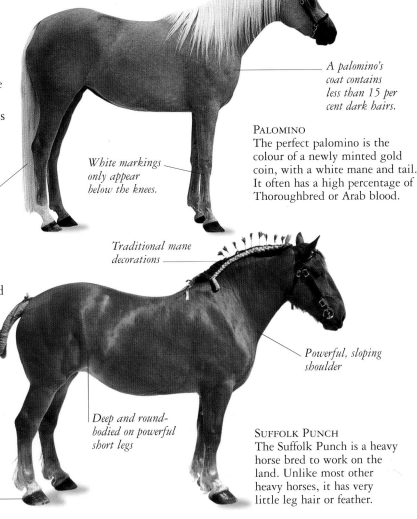

Arab influence is often noticeable in tail.

White markings only appear below the knees.

A palomino's coat contains less than 15 per cent dark hairs.

PALOMINO
The perfect palomino is the colour of a newly minted gold coin, with a white mane and tail. It often has a high percentage of Thoroughbred or Arab blood.

Breed colours

Suffolk Punches and Cleveland Bays are always the same colour. The Cleveland Bay is always bay, and the Suffolk Punch is always one of seven shades of chestnut. If either breed is crossed with a Thoroughbred, the colour is often, but not always, passed on.

Traditional mane decorations

Powerful, sloping shoulder

Deep and round-bodied on powerful short legs

Round, hard hooves are smaller than many heavy breeds.

SUFFOLK PUNCH
The Suffolk Punch is a heavy horse bred to work on the land. Unlike most other heavy horses, it has very little leg hair or feather.

Pattern variations

Appaloosas and Pintos both have a number of recognized coat patterns. Appaloosas are either leopard, blanket, snowflake, marble, or frost. Leopards have white backs and hips with dark spots. White blankets are white over the hips. Snowflakes have widespread dark spots, marbles have mottled body colouring, and frosts have dark coats with white flecks. Pintos have two coat patterns – tobianos have white areas that start from the top of the body and extend down. White overos have white areas that start from the lower body.

LEOPARD PATTERN

Leopard pattern has large, dark spots.

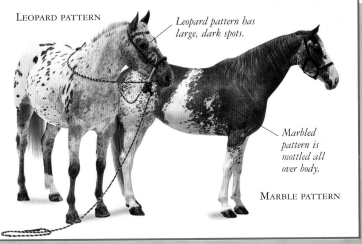

Marbled pattern is mottled all over body.

MARBLE PATTERN

GAITED HORSES

MOST HORSES and ponies have four natural gaits; walk, trot, canter, and gallop. However, some breeds have special gaits and are known as gaited horses. These gaits make the horses particularly comfortable to ride or look spectacular in harness. A gait is a natural characteristic of a particular breed, but may be encouraged and exaggerated with special training.

Traditionally shown with long, flowing manes and tails.

COMFORTABLE RIDE
Tennessee Walking horses are said to be the most comfortable of all riding horses. The breed is calm and kind, which makes it suitable for beginner and experienced riders alike.

Tennessee Walking horse

The Tennessee Walking horse originated in the southern states of the US and has Spanish ancestry. This breed looks quite ordinary when standing still, but its smooth, gliding gaits make it look very special when moving. It has three gaits; a flat or ordinary walk, a running walk, and a rocking horse canter.

Long, elegant neck helps horse to balance.

Low head carriage

Long, sloping shoulder make horse comfortable to ride.

Black and chestnut are the most popular colours for performance horses.

Coat can be any colour, but solid colours are seen most often.

Hind feet have long heels to accentuate the smooth action of the gaits.

Front hooves are deliberately kept longer than usual and often shod with weighted shoes to exaggerate the action of the gaits.

Tail is set far up on the quarters and is carried high naturally.

The Paso can trot at 26 kmph (16 mph) while still giving a smooth ride.

At rest the Hackney should stand square, with its front legs straight and hindlegs back.

Hackney

The high-stepping Hackney is famous for its flamboyant trot. It is uncomfortable to ride, but makes a spectacular driving horse. There are Hackney ponies, which stand up to 14 hh, and Hackney horses, which reach about 15.3 hh.

Peruvian Paso

The Paso descends from horses brought to Peru by 16th century Spanish explorers. The Paso can canter, but is best known for its trot. Its three trots are called Paso Corto, Paso Fino, and Paso Largo; ordinary, slow, and fast.

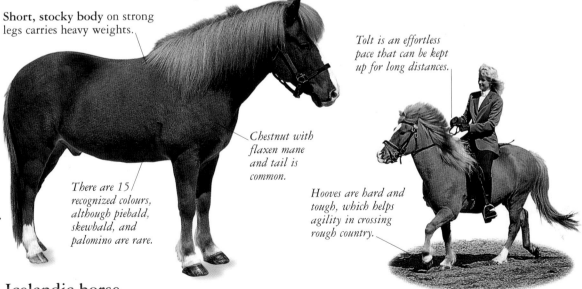

Short, stocky body on strong legs carries heavy weights.

Chestnut with flaxen mane and tail is common.

There are 15 recognized colours, although piebald, skewbald, and palomino are rare.

Tolt is an effortless pace that can be kept up for long distances.

Hooves are hard and tough, which helps agility in crossing rough country.

Icelandic horse

Although the Icelandic horse never stands more than 13.2 hh and is often smaller, it is always called a horse and never a pony. It is very strong for its size and is ridden by adults, even in races.

TOLT
The Icelandic horse has five natural gaits. The most famous is the tolt, a running walk that is used to cross uneven ground at speed.

HORSES FOR HERDSMEN

HORSES AND HERDSMEN have always been natural partners. A rider on a trained horse can herd sheep, cattle, and even other horses, while people on foot or in motor vehicles would fail. Some breeds, such as the Camargue horse and the Quarter horse, have been developed especially for herding. A good herdsman's horse is fast and agile and learns to anticipate its rider's next command.

Rounding up sheep

Wherever sheep are kept, horses and ponies are used to move them from one place to another. The Australian Stock horse, Exmoor pony, and Welsh Cob are all perfect for this type of work.

Australian Stock horses have Thoroughbred-type heads; others, with Quarter horse blood, have squarer faces.

Fine mane shows Thoroughbred and Arab influence.

Stockmen may ride with one hand.

Powerful shoulder and long neck help horse to keep its balance at speed and when making sharp turns.

Strong legs

Tough, hard hooves

AUSTRALIAN STOCK HORSE
The Australian Stock horse has Thoroughbred and Arab blood, and is usually between 15 and 16.2 hh. It descends from horses brought to New South Wales about 200 years ago.

STAMINA AND ENDURANCE
Australian sheep station workers cover long distances in high temperatures. Their horses do not have to be fast, but do need plenty of stamina and great endurance.

Work and play

The early American settlers used their cattle horses in harness and for entertainment. The favourite sports were sprint races over short distances and cattle cutting competitions.

Muscular hindquarters for turning power

CUTTING HORSES
A herd rider often has to single out one cow or calf from the rest of the herd. This activity is called cutting. Many good cutting horses are Quarter horses and they are highly prized for their abilities.

QUARTER HORSE
The Quarter horse was used for work and sport. It was traditionally raced over a quarter of a mile, which is how it got its name.

Joints must be strong to take stress of sharp turns and halts.

Herding cows

In some parts of France, the US, Australia, and other countries, horses are still used to round up cattle. Camargue horses bred in France, herd wild black bulls, which can be fierce and aggressive.

Thick tail for protection against flies

Halters, made from twisted horsehair, are worn by Camargue horses.

CAMARGUE HORSE
Although the Camargue horse only stands between 13.2 and 14.2 hh, it is always called a horse rather than a pony and is very powerful. The Camargue horses have lived wild in the Rhône delta for over a thousand years.

AMERICAN COWBOYS
Although there are few true cowboys today, some horses are still used to round up cattle. Cowboys need horses that are both intelligent and well trained.

WILD HORSES

TODAY THERE IS only one truly wild horse – Przewalski's horse. However, there are many other types and breeds, such as the Mustangs from western America and the Brumbies from Australia, that are often called wild but are in fact feral. These horses have ancestors that were domesticated but later escaped into the wild, where they formed herds. Wild and feral horses have to survive on poor quality and often scarce grazing.

Stallions will fight others if provoked.

RUNNING WILD
Horse herds consist of mares, foals, and young horses. Each herd is led by a stallion, which defends the territory, and there is also a lead mare that dominates the other mares.

Feral horses

Wild and feral horses are often resented by farmers because they graze on land needed for livestock. Mustangs are protected by law in the US and some are caught and domesticated to try and safeguard the future of the breed.

Zebras and asses

Zebras and asses belong to the same family as the horse. All are related to *Pliohippus*, the first horse ancestor to run on one toe. The African wild ass is the relative of the domesticated donkey. There are several different species of zebra including the common zebra, and Grevy's zebra.

Every zebra has a unique striped pattern.

An ass, when crossed with a horse produces a mule.

Some Mustangs have dark stripes, called eel stripes, that run down their backs.

MUSTANG
The Mustang descends from the Spanish horse and its name comes from a Spanish word, "mestena", which means a herd of horses. The Mustang was the foundation for many of the American breeds and has retained many Spanish characteristics, especially its colour.

Hard hooves are essential for survival when covering large areas of land.

Narrow body generally lacks muscle.

Sable Island ponies

Sable Island is an island off Nova Scotia, Canada. It is home to a herd of about 250 wild ponies descended from ancestors that are supposed to have swum ashore from a wrecked ship in the 17th century.

Przewalski's horse

Przewalski's horse was found roaming wild on the plains of Mongolia in the late 19th century. It has a bristly mane and a light coloured muzzle and is the only truly wild horse in the world. Today Przewalski's horses are not found in the wild, but can be seen in zoos. Scientists have plans to return a herd to the wild.

Elegant neck and head reveals Spanish ancestry.

Powerful shoulder adds speed needed for survival in the wild.

Fine coats due to Thoroughbred blood

BRUMBIES

Australian Brumbies are descended from domesticated horses, which were turned loose in the 19th century. Brumbies are similar in type to Australian Stock horses. Like Mustangs, they are tough and hardy but unpopular with farmers since they graze on farm land.

Brumbies exist on sparse grazing and travel miles to find water.

HORSE AND PONY CHART

THIS CHART GIVES you an overall view of all
the horses and ponies mentioned in this book.
Use it as a quick-reference guide to look up
the differences between each breed or type.

TYPES

COB	HUNTER	HUNTER	POLO PONY	RIDING HORSE
• Any colour, usually grey • Up to 15.3 hh • Riding and driving		• Any colour • Around 16 – 16.2 hh • Hunting	• Any colour • Around 15.1 hh • Polo matches	• Any colour • Up to 15 – 16.2 hh • All types of riding

LIGHT

ANDALUCIAN	ANGLO-ARAB	APPALOOSA	APPALOOSA	ARAB
• Bay, shades of grey, mulberry • Around 15.2 hh • Dressage, parade riding	• Chestnut, bay, brown • 15 – 16.3 hh • All riding sports	• Black, brown, chestnut and white • 14.2 – 15.2 hh • Western riding, all sports		• Any solid colour • 14.2 – 15 hh • Endurance, racing
AUSTRALIAN STOCK • Any solid colour • 15 – 16.2 hh • Herding sheep and cattle, general riding	BAVARIAN WARMBLOOD • Any solid colour • Around 16 hh • All sports	CLEVELAND BAY • Bay • 16 – 16.2 hh • Riding, driving		DANISH WARMBLOOD • Any solid colour • 16.1 – 16.2 hh • Dressage, showjumping
DUTCH WARMBLOOD • Any colour, bay and brown most common • 15.2 – 16.2 hh • Showjumping, dressage	HACKNEY • Dark brown, black, bay, chestnut • 15 – 15.3 hh • Driving	HANOVERIAN • Any solid colour • 15.3 – 16.2 hh • Dressage, showjumping	ICELANDIC HORSE • Chestnut, dun, bay, grey, black • 12.3 – 13.2 hh • Riding, all sports	IRISH DRAUGHT • Any solid colour • 15.2 – 17 hh • Showjumping, all riding, hunting
LIPIZZANER • Grey • 15.1 – 16.2 hh • Dressage, driving	LUSITANO • Any colour, mainly grey • 15 – 16 hh • Dressage	PERUVIAN PASO • Any colour, mainly bay and chestnut • 14 – 15 hh • Riding	QUARTER HORSE • Any solid colour, mainly chestnut • 14.3 – 16 hh • Riding, racing, herding, cutting	SELLE FRANÇAIS • Any colour, mainly chestnut • 15.2 – 16.2 hh • Dressage, eventing, showjumping
SHAGYA ARAB • Any solid colour, mainly grey • Around 15 hh • Riding	STANDARDBRED • Any solid colour • Around 15.2 hh • Harness racing, endurance	TENNESSEE WALKING • Black and solid colours • 15 – 16 hh • Riding	THOROUGHBRED • Any solid colour • 15 – 16.2 hh • Racing, eventing	TRAKEHNER • Any solid colour • 16 – 16.2 hh • Dressage, showjumping

WILD AND FERAL

BRUMBIES	CAMARGUE	MUSTANG		PRZEWALSKI'S HORSE
• All colours • 15 – 16.2 hh • Australia	• Grey • 13.1 – 14.1 hh • France	• All colours • 13.2 – 15 hh • United States	MUSTANG	• Dun • Around 14.3 hh • Mongolia

HEAVY

BELGIAN DRAUGHT • Bay, dun, grey, red-roan • 16.2 – 17 hh • Farm work	**CLYDESDALE** • Bay, brown, grey, black, roan • 16.2 – 17 hh • Farm work	CLYDESDALE	**FRIESIAN** • Black • Around 15 hh • Driving, riding
PERCHERON • Dapple-grey, black • 16 – 17 hh • Farm work	**SHIRE** • Black, bay, brown, grey • 16.2 – 17.2 hh • Farm work		**SUFFOLK PUNCH** • Shades of chestnut • 16 – 16.3 hh • Farm work

PONIES

AMERCAN SHETLAND • Brown, black, bay, chestnut, roan cream, dun, grey • 103 cm (42 in) • Driving	**BARDIGIANO** • Bay, brown • Up to 13.3 hh • Riding, farm work	**BASHKIR** • Red chestnut, bay, light brown • Around 14 hh • Riding, driving, kept for milk	**CASPIAN** • Bay, grey, chestnut, black, cream • 10 – 12 hh • Child's riding	**CONNEMARA** • Usually grey • 13 – 14.2 hh • Riding, driving
DARTMOOR • Bay, black, brown • Around 12.2 hh • Child's riding, driving	**DALES** • Black, bay, brown • Up to 14.2 hh • Farm work, trekking	**EXMOOR** • Bay, brown, dun • 12.2 – 12.3 hh • Riding	**FALABELLA** • Any colour • 76 cm (30 in) • Pet only	 FALABELLA
FELL • Black, brown, bay, grey • Up to 14 hh • Riding, driving	**FJORD** • Dun • 13 – 14 hh • Riding	**HAFLINGER** • Chestnut, palomino • Up to 13.3 hh • Driving	**HIGHLAND** • Dun, grey, brown, black, bay • Up to 14.2 hh • Riding, driving, packhorse	**LANDAIS** • Any colour • 11.3 – 13.1 hh • Riding
 FELL — NEW FOREST		**NEW FOREST** • Any colour except piebald and skewbald • 14.2 hh • Riding, driving	**PONY OF THE AMERICAS** • Black, brown, chestnut and white • 11.2 – 13.2 hh • Child's riding	**POTTOK** • Any colour • 11.1 – 14.2 hh • Riding, farm work
SHETLAND • Any colour except piebald and skewbald • 101 cm (40 in) • Child's riding, driving	**TIMOR** • Bay, black, brown • 9 – 11 hh • Riding, farm work	**WELSH SECTION A** • Any colour except piebald and skewbald • Up to 12 hh • Riding, driving		
WELSH SECTION B • Any colour except piebald and skewbald • Up to 13.2 hh • Riding, driving	**WELSH SECTION C** • Any colour except piebald and skewbald • 13.2 hh • Riding, driving, trekking	**WELSH SECTION D** • Any colour except piebald and skewbald • Over 13.2 hh • Riding, driving	POTTOK	

GLOSSARY

THERE ARE LOTS of words that are used specifically to describe horses and their habits. Some have been used throughout this book and can be found, with a description of their meaning, below.

BLOOD Used to describe a horse's breeding. A blood horse is another term for a Thoroughbred.

BRAND An identifying mark made on the skin of a horse.

BREED Horses or ponies with the same ancestry. Breeds develop over many years and horses of the same breed share the same physical characteristics.

CANNON BONE The part of the foreleg between the knee and the fetlock.

CARRIAGE HORSE A term used to describe a lightly-built harness horse.

COACH HORSE A harness horse able to pull heavy coaches.

COLDBLOODS Another term for heavy horse breeds.

COMPETITION HORSE Horse that is bred and trained to compete in a particular activity.

CONFORMATION The shape of a horse's body and legs. Good conformation means the horse is well-proportioned.

CONSTITUTION Physical make-up, structure of a horse

CROSSBREED A horse or pony that is the result of crossing one breed with another breed or type.

DISHED HEAD A head with a concave profile, such as the Arab.

DRESSAGE Training which helps the horse to become supple and athletic.

DRIVING HORSE Horse that is bred to pull a cart or carriage.

ENDURANCE HORSE A horse that competes in long-distance rides. Most top endurance horses are Arab, partbred Arab, or Standardbred.

EVENTER A horse that is trained to compete in horse trials, or eventing.

FERAL HORSE Horse whose ancestors were domesticated, but which now roams in the wild.

FOREARM The top of the foreleg down to the knee.

FORELEGS The front legs.

FRAME The structure of a horse.

FREEZE MARK A painless security marking system where the horse is cold branded with a unique combination of letters and numbers.

FROG Sensitive, V-shaped underneath part of the hoof which acts as a shock absorber.

GAIT The pattern of a horse's footsteps.

GELDING A male horse that can no longer reproduce.

GIRTH The measurement round a horse's body where the girth rests.

HAND A unit of measurement to describe a horse's height at the withers. A hand is 10 cm (4 in).

HARNESS An arrangement of straps fitted to a horse so that it can be attached to a cart.

HH Abbreviation for hands high.

HINDQUARTERS The back end of a horse, including the hindlegs.

HOCKS Powerful joints halfway down the hindleg.

HOTBLOOD Another term for a Thoroughbred or Arab horse or one with a high percentage of Thoroughbred or Arab blood. The opposite of coldblood.

LOINS The lower part of a horse's back, just in front of the quarters.

MARE A female horse more than four years old.

MARKINGS The arrangement of colours on a horse's coat.

PARTBRED A horse of known cross breeding.

PASTERNS The portion of a horse's leg between the fetlock and the hoof.

POINTS The external parts of a horse that make up its conformation. Also used to describe the tips of the ears, mane, tail, and lower legs.

PUREBRED A pure strain of horse from many generations of controlled breeding.

STALLION A male horse that is used for breeding.

SURE-FOOTED Unlikely to stumble.

TYPE A horse that fulfils a particular purpose, but does not necessarily have known breeding.

WARMBLOODS In general, partbred Arab or Thoroughbred horses. Specifically, there are warmblood breeds such as the Hanoverian and Dutch warmblood that have been carefully bred to produce ideal modern sports horses.

INDEX

ACKNOWLEDGMENTS

Dorling Kindersley would like to thank the following people for their help in the production of this book.

The author
Carolyn Henderson has lived and worked with horses for many years. She is a regular contributor to specialist magazines such as *Horse and Hound*, and has written and edited a variety of books on all aspects of keeping, riding, and training horses.

The publishers would also like to thank Hilary Bird for the index, Janine Amos for editorial assistance, and Darren Holt, Cheryl Telfer, and Ann Thompson for design assistance. CAM Equestrian Ltd, Eardisley, Hereford for providing images of jumping poles.

The author wishes acknowledge Elwyn Hartley Edwards for his extensive knowledge of horse and pony breeds.

Picture Credits
The publishers would like to thank the following people for their kind permission to reproduce their photographs.
key: *b* bottom, *c* centre, *l* left, *t* top, *r* right

Animal Photography/Sally Anne Thompson: 27*br;* 33*tr;*
Bridgeman Art Library, London & N.Y/Roy Miles Gallery, London: 18*t* (Sir Edwin Landseer, *Arab Stallion*); **J. Allan Cash Ltd:** 36*t* Bruce Coleman Ltd: 42*bc;*
Kit Houghton: 2; 14-15*t;* 17*tr;* 20*t;* 40*br;* 41*tl;* 39*tr;* **Bob Langrish:** 6-7; 16*bl;* 21*t;* 30*br;* 32*t;* 35*tr;* 38*t;* 39*br;* 42*t;* 43*t, br;*

Pictor International: 14*t;* 41*br;* **Frank Spooner Pictures:** 17*tl;* 19*t* (*Gamma,* Alain Benainous).

Additional photography
Other photographey was taken by Philip Dowell, Mary Evans, Kit Houghton, Colin Keates, Bob Langrish, Karl Shone, Jerry Young, Berwick Woodcuts.
The publishers would also like to thank all horse and ponies we photographed, their owners. These are as follows.
Cover: Mr and Mrs Dimmock; Moscow Hippodrome, USSR; Haras, National de Compiegne; **Page 8-9:** *Taws Little Buck,* Kentucky Horse Park; *Fruich of Dykes,* Countess of Swindon; *Fakir Bola,* Moscow Hippodrome, Russia; *Murrayton Delphinlis,* June Freeman, Murrayton Stud, UK; *Hopstone Shabdiz,* Mrs Scott, Henden Caspian Stud, UK;
Page 10-11: *Hit   man,* Boyd Cantrell, Kentucky Horse Park, USA; **Page 14-15:** *Brutt,* Robert Oliver, UK; *Superted ,* Robert Oliver, UK; *Hobo,* Robert Oliver, UK; *Amoco Park,* Spruce Meadows, Canada (also p22-23); **Page 22-23:** *Rambling Willie,* Farrington Stables & the estate of Paul Siebert; Kentucky Horse Park, USA.
Page 24-25: *Barlin,* Moscow Agricultural Academy, Russia; *Chatsworth Belle;* Mrs Hampton, Briar Stud, UK; *Fruich of Dykes,* Countess of Swinton; *Allendale Vampire;* Miss M Houlden, Havenstud, UK; *Waverhead-William,* Mr & Mrs Errington, UK; **Page 26-27:** *Tressor des Pins,* Haras de Pall, France; *Ausdan Svejk,* John Goddard Fenwick & Lyn Moran,

Dyfed, UK; *Orchidea,* Sadamo Tombini, Perego, Italy; Page 28-29 *Hopstone Shabdiz,* Mrs Scott, Henden Caspian Stud, UK; *Pegasus of Kilverstone,* Lady Fischer, Kilverstone Wildlife Park, UK; *Meriam Beluna,* Peltia Jaya Stable, Jakarta, Indonesia; *Mels Lucky Boy,* Mr D Stewart, Kentucky Horse Park, USA; **Page 30-31:** *Edison,* Mrs Dejonge; *Soir d'Avril,* Haras Nationaux de l'Isle de Lion d'Angers; **Page 32-33:** *Miss Mill,* Mr R J Lampard; *Oaten Mainbrace,* Mr & Mrs Dimock, UK; **Page 34-35:** *Tango,* Haras National de Saint Lo, France; *Roy;* Kentucky Horse Park, USA; **Page 36-37:** *Golden Nugget,* Sally Chaplin, UK; *Laurel Keepsake II,* P. Adams and Sons, Laurel Farm, UK; **Page 38-39:** *Leikner,* Kentucky Horse Park, USA; *Delights Moondus,* Andrew and Jane Shan, Kentucky Horse Park, USA; **Page 40-41** *Mr Starpasser,* Pat Butcher, Canada; *Redounet,* Mr Contreras, Les Saintes Maries de la Mer, France.

Useful addresses
Here are the addresses of some societies and other organizations that you may like to contact.

British Horse Society, The
British Equestrian Centre
Stoneleigh Deer Park
Kenilworth
Warwickshire
CV8 2XZ
Tel: 01926 707700

National Pony Society
Willingdon House
102 High Street
Alton, Hants
GU34 1EN
Tel: 01420 8833

Ponies Association UK
Chesham House
56 Green End Road
Sawtry
Huntingdon
Cambridgeshire PE17 5XA
Tel: 01487 830278

Pony Club, The
The British Equestrian Centre
Stoneleigh Deer Park
Kenilworth
Warwickshire CV8 2XZ
Tel: 01926 707700

Equestrian Federaton of Australia
196 Greenhill Road
Eastwood
SA 5063, Australia
Tel: (08) 8357 0077

Equestrian Federation Saddle Horse Council
70 Falters Road
Wilberforce
NSW 2756, Australia
Tel: (02) 4575 1341